Mental Health Writing

How writing helps your mental health

Jason Pegler and Chipmunka authors

chipmunkapublishing
the mental health publisher

All rights reserved, no part of this publication may be reproduced by any means, electronic, mechanical photocopying, documentary, film or in any other format without prior written permission of the publisher.

>Published by
>Chipmunkapublishing
>United Kingdom

http://www.chipmunkapublishing.com

Copyright © 2019 Each author owns their own copyright. Copyright of the anthology as a published book is with the publisher.

ISBN   978-1-78382-470-0

I am delighted, grateful and honoured to have commissioned this book by fantastic mental health writers around the world. In 2002 I set up Chipmunkapublishing to give a voice to mental health writers around the world after writing my own memoir on living with manic depression entitled "A Can of Madness". Writing that memoir was both the most painful and the most cathartic thing that I ever did. Writing saved my life and enabled me to create a new future for myself. I no longer had to be defined by my past once I had accepted what happened to me. I've written many books over the years including "Curing Madness", "The Ultimate Guide To Well Being", "Mental Health Raps", "Mental Health Publishing and Empowerment", "Mental Health Coaching" and "Long Distance Triathlon Memoir". By 2019 I will have published 700 authors and over 1100 different titles with the help of my amazing Chipmunka team both past and present.

Since 2002 I have seen familiar patterns with other writers who have experienced mental illness. We all enjoy writing. Writing helps all of us in similar and different ways. Writing is escapism, a process, mindfulness, and creativity; mirroring, joy, confrontation and a never-ending tool that can keep over active minds occupied and lift saddened minds from the depths of despair. Like most writers I have started many more books than I have finished. I've run Creative Writing Workshops on Positivity to encourage happier writing and also made MP's on "How To Write a Book and Stop Procrastinating" (Free on our website www.chipmunkapublishing.com by the way). I once heard a wise man say that there is no such thing as writers block. Just write. There is an element of truth in that. The talent on show in this book amazes me. Practically everyone in it has been published by Chipnunkapublishing at some time or other. I hope they will continue to be part of the history of the mental health publishing genre that we are documenting. I am overwhelmed by the poignancy, insight, creativity, diversity and variety in people's work.

We all love writing in this book and I hope this comes across to the reader. We also all write in order to help our mental health in some way or other.

Jason Pegler

February 2019

'At the Intersection of Poetry and Mental Health'

A Speech Given for a Panel at the Flem-Ken Festival of Arts and Ideas
On the 27th of October, 2018

Paul Fearne

Welcome. What has poetry got to do with mental health? Well everything.

Madness has long been associated with poetry. Let us consider an old saying – "He had neither rhyme nor reason". In this aphorism there lies a great truth. It is acceptable in society to have one, or the other, but never lacking in both! Let us unpack this further. If one has reason, one is happily accepted into society. But if one lacks this attribute, then one must, by necessity, have rhyme! And what does this mean? One must be a poet, whose principle mode of engagement in the world was through rhyme, at the time the saying was coined. So reason yes, and if no to that, then rhyme. A trouble begins for the individual if they have neither!

So one can lack reason, and still be happily accepted into society, if they have rhyme; vis-à-vis poetry. In essence, a person can be mad, but if they have poetry, they gain entry into society just as surely as the person who has only reason. As I said, an important truth lies in this old saying. So a diagnosis comes, let us say schizophrenia. And here, a person's life flashes before their eyes. Who me, like THEM? Maybe they have been hospitalised, or maybe if they are lucky, seen by a private clinician. But this is not the end, but the very beginning. What can I do from here?

The answer is a simple one. Start writing. This is what I did. During my first episode I kept a diary. Years went by, and I became well again. I did a masters and a PhD, and I kept writing poetry, and eventually got some things published. Then at the end of my PhD, I dusted off the diary, and sent it to a publisher, who rejected it. Then to another, and success! Then, by an act of fate I saw a call for submissions to the Melbourne Writers Festival, who accepted the book, to be launched there. Natasha Mitchel from Radio National picked up the story, and I was interviewed on her show. I was still writing poetry, and some was read on Natasha's show. I hit the poetry scene, and did readings, and was a feature at the Dan O'Connell! All because I wrote.

So poetry, writing – this is the way to overcome your illness. You may become ill again, just as I did, but because I wrote I was contributing to society. At times I had no reason, but I had rhyme. So through this I carried on, and won a great victory against my illness. It would not conquer me, I had conquered it. I had rhyme!

There is a history in letters as they relate to madness. Friedrich Holderlin, living in 18th century Germany was to succumb to a schizophrenic-like break with reality, but before he did, he left us a truly modern corpus of fragmented poetry. Antonin Artaud was a film star in the silent era, before he gave it up to pursue poetry and writing. He had schizophrenia, and was hospitalised in France during the German occupation of the Second World War. August Strindberg, more of a playwright, was known for such plays as 'Miss Julie' and 'A Dream Play', suffered very similar symptoms to schizophrenia. There was Ezra Pound, Janet Frame, and Sylvia Plath, and a whole gamut of sufferers who used the poetic capacities in their respective conditions to create great works.

My advice is this – if you suffer from a mental illness, write. It is a grand tradition that will see you accepted into society, and if you are lucky, even revered. It is in every one with a mental illness to create great things. We are fortunate that we have this avenue open to us. Things go from being grim, to a wonderful opportunity. People who are sane do not write as good poetry as those who are ill. Poetry, it will transform your life. And give you things you could never expect. Poetry.

Let us look at an example from schizophrenia. There is a phenomenon in schizophrenia called 'looseness of association'. In this phenomenon, normal speech, which relies on a tightness of association, is derailed. An apple, which can normally be associated with 'pip' or 'core', can now be associated with 'bread' or 'drum'. It goes into a further phenomenon called a word salad, where things that would not normally go together do. Much frustration for the listener, but not for one important thing – poetry. Poetry relies upon unusual associations, and the more unusual the better. Let us look at an example - the dawn, a common trope in poetry. But how do we make this clichéd device new and novel to our modern ears? Rather than the 'rising of the dawn', or 'dawn breaks', we might have 'the floating of the dawn', or the 'seething of the dawn'. This move requires us to see the dawn differently through an act of loosening of association. The history of poetry depends on this move. And the masters of this move are those suffering from schizophrenia.

There is a further thing implicit in mental illness that lends itself to great poetry. And that is suffering. It has long helped me and my suffering to believe that suffering in some way helps the creative capacities of the individual. Whenever I experience suffering, I simply write. It is a great outlet, and a great way to manage the suffering you go through, to channel it into creative pursuits. And who experiences a lot of suffering - people who live through mental illness. If the premise of this argument is true, and that suffering is conducive to creativity, then who better to create great works than those suffering from mental illness. I might add a caveat here, that we need not seek out suffering if we have a mental illness, there is enough here already!

And what if things get really grim, and you are hospitalised! Keep writing is the key. I once saw a title for a book, and it was called something like, 'Poems from the Madhouse'. It can actually help your career no end to have had the experience of being hospitalised – street cred as it were. I once had a launch for a book at Readings on the Melbourne University Campus, a store that is no longer there, unfortunately. But the time came around for the launch, and I was hospitalised at Royal Melbourne, John Cade. They gave me permission to attend the launch, so I went! There was no one there, except me, my carer from John Cade, the person launching the book, and the person who was running the store. Not to be deterred, I read my speech, and the person who launching the book read theirs. They even let me have a glass of wine! Now that was a launch! Street cred!

So my advice to you, if you have a mental illness – write, and in particular, write poetry. It will give you direction when you really need it. And read poetry too! Take up the pen; it is mightier than your illness!

A few vignettes from my life can help set the tone. I have spent a lot of my life well, but there are times when I have been unwell, and indeed hospitalised. Some very amusing things have happened during these times. The first time I was hospitalised, I came to the hospital saying I was a famous writer! Ha! Like all schizophrenics, of course. In actual fact I had just launched my Diary of a Schizophrenic at the Melbourne Writers Festival, and had been interviewed on Radio National's show 'All in the Mind' with Natasha Mitchell! So I guess I was more 'well-known' than famous, but still, I wasn't far off!

In hospital, I attempted to get one of the nurses to call me 'doctor', which she wouldn't. I said to her, 'that took me 6 years of hard work' – but she still wouldn't!

When I was first admitted to John Cade, I was interviewed by a team of psychiatrists. They asked me what medication I was on. I straight away asked, 'What medication are you on?' This stemmed from a hunch that sometimes psychiatrists have their own battles with mental illness, and can be on medication as well!

What is it about these stories that help? It is their adventurous quality. I am a big believer in adventure. You sort of have to be to get by as someone with a mental illness. With mental illness, life is an unbelievably large adventure. There are things you can't control, but if you just keep going, you encounter what I call 'safe levels', where you can enjoy the view for a brief time, before moving on to the next part of the adventure, whether that be illness or health. It is really up to you, which one it is. Medication is a key here. If you choose to take your medication, then wellness can be yours, and great lengths of times stretch ahead for writing, and forming friendships, have fun, and enjoying life. If you chose it, it can be yours!

What has poetry got to do with this – well everything. I once coined a saying of my own; it went – 'It matters not what afflicts you, as long as you have a witticism at hand, and a story to relate afterward'. And this is true of a poet more than any other adventurer. All one must do is read a biography of Lord Byron to see the truth of this. Sometimes we make suffering happen, sometimes it is thrust upon us. But in the end, if we have the quill, we will beat our respective illnesses into a right submission!

Jamie Kershaw

Writing as Catharsis   -   Why do you write?

Writing is magical! To be creative and artistic requires that, in writing, we can create a unique world and immerse other people in it. I write to communicate and also to get things off my chest. God granted me a purpose in life; by this means I feel at ease with family, music and writing – kind of a way towards some sort of community contribution, and the power of knowledge for others. I'm not as good at verbalising and processing information as I am when writing. Contributing to something bigger than myself (i.e. the literary community) means that Art is at its best when it's telling stories – either yours or someone else's. It resonates – good stories and good art connect with people on an emotional level – not always the most demonstrably technically proficient work. It's the realisation of experiences that otherwise wouldn't be possible.

How does it help you relax/self-improve?

Intellectual security. Things often seem more overwhelming before they're written down. Does it help mindfulness? There's a good argument for both helping mindfulness and not being about mindfulness at all.....*Writing as something to focus on* allows you to create a world where it's safe to tell your stories without being explicit. How does it help creativity? The question answers itself, as a way to direct all of that extra energy into something practical and a place to house it.

What genre do you write?

With Chipmunka we have four published projects, beginning with a Fiction novel, going to Mental Health Non-Fiction Research via two Biographical accounts (also Non-Fiction). *Plan 103f* is currently going through a transformational 2nd edition. This Fiction Novel is the first part of the *Squirrels of Destiny* Trilogy Project. 'Squirrels of Destiny' being part two. The third part is yet to be written. *Plan 103f* was written on a creative trajectory, and as a way to realise various hopes, dreams and aspirations via fictitious characters. On the other hand, *MIND Matters* consists of detailed research; interviews, movie reviews, literature, a Consultant Psychiatrist, a mother-son conversation, and the conclusions uncover 16 brand new 'connecting factors' between Asperger's Syndrome, Borderline Personality Disorder, and Schizophrenia. This was written as a way of conveying experiences lived through in my twenties.

Grandpa Billy tells the life story of George William Kershaw in a 20th Century historical context. Written as a tribute by amanuensis, *Grandpa Billy (1901-1993)* lived through a broken family background, disjointed education, Two World Wars – serving on German POW Farm camps in WW1, and the RAF Ground Crew for the Biggin Hill Spitfires in WW2. Billy was also a talented Dance Band Banjoist, and through the 1950s-60s worked as a Semi-Skilled Engineering Supervisor at Jowett Car Factory in Bradford. With periods in Bradford, Manchester, and Shropshire, Billy certainly saw his fair share of life's challenges.

The other biographical account is something of which I owe the entire literary community a deep apology. The Green Dragon is Non-Fiction. Charting my life from birth up to the age of 32 years. With a certain emphasis on family, friends, music, historical context and mental health, *The Green Dragon* is a matter of fact account of certain life experiences – but without too much emotional content, or feelings discussed. Right now *The Green Dragon* is nearly ten years out of date, and again I apologise for seeing this account published when it was. I feel that the right to do so should logically have waited at least a further 5-10 years. But – as they say – *'Retrospect is a marvellous thing!'*

Two future pieces include *'Short Works'* consisting of Poetry, Children's Stories, Essays, Travel Adventures, and a Small Business Blueprint. This is work-in-progress. Also, a book about music co-written with a friend. We are provisionally aiming for 2025+ for this release. These and a handful of very short, but witty and concise Children's Stories are the genres I have explored thus far. Searching for an Illustrator!

So *Carpe Diem! Seize the Day!* Writing is indeed magical. We can escape into a world of our own creation. Somewhere to feel safe in an ever changing, and crazy, crazy world. Literature, Culture and Art form a complete picture. It is our moral responsibility as writers to add to, extend and coherently contribute to this world as best we are able!

Karl Lorenz Willett

I have been unfortunate to have the disease Paranoid Schizophrenia, I have made this disguised blessing very much a part of whom I am and was fortunate throughout my life to write about sad, depressed and also despairing times and the pride, joy and also happiness with which I have been blessed. I chronicle the failures to successes and I wrote of the rich emotional conflicts that came from out-of-control positive symptoms punishing the self and also wrote about the negative symptoms and the lack of cognition decline inefficiency. I feel reward for helping people without mental illnesses to have a depth of feelings, which enable them to mentalize the impairment in my mind, which were my lived experiences.

Writing gives me values, it also lifts my mood and puts me in a unique position where people shower me with praise and attribute qualities that seem to me almost verging on the divine, because they feel it's a big deal that I am a writer. My modesty does not allow me to brag because writing is very useful for me to lay down learning in my mind and re-reading sets it like concrete. Writing gives me entertainment along the way; when life is taken as having challenges one can have a laugh when writing then down, but it's much too difficult to laugh when there are problems. I am self-educating myself about schizophrenia as I write and knowledge for readers so, they could understand about mental illnesses better and understand them well. Then discussion can move forward to break down barriers rooted in prejudice, avoidance, rejection, and discrimination, which are due to a lack of understanding and if it's not tackled cause sufferers to internalize social myths and prejudices and experience self-stigma.

My reason to write has many functions and its not always about communicating my ideas, feelings and inner beliefs. I want to know about you, you and you.... all of you and my language make me think in words to change the wrong ideas in communities about mental illness, demons, supernatural, devil, evil, suffering and the afterlife, so as to counter fear, social stereotypes and challenge your own assumptions about those things.

My writing is aimed to interfere with and change the thinking between heads to avoid using stigmatizing language, and to fully support each other, protect each other and value each other. When I write I am operating at my most sophisticated level which may be at a part of frontier of knowledge about schizophrenia and I also think about the world in a very different way, probably thinking stuff nobody has thought of or experienced as I have. I have been writing about stuff since 1982 and using the writing process to help myself think. The thinking I am doing feels it is at the level of such complexity that I have to use writing to help myself do the thinking and only edit the words after re-reading. I am writing these messages of my thinking to readers and if readers read my messages they may change the way they see the world and schizophrenics.

As readers you may be able to read the pattern of my writing language and stop reading before I have interfered in your own thinking processes. But you may not understand the message I want to put over and become aggregated (*agitated?*).

Writing is one way I use to record my ideas and experiences as I strive to my ideal. Ideas and experiences are not written to be preserved indefinitely, but to move knowledge on and our spaces forward by changing people's attitudes, discriminatory thoughts about disability, so that all of us can participate in this great world no matter what flaws or imperfections we may have. I hope that my writing will be of value for readers to change bad ideology in privileged heads before they cause havoc when played out on the species on the planet. The twentieth century had many examples of this and very little has changed - it's now the **year 2018**. I believe that extraordinary common people without violence must begin to find ways to manipulate the minds of the stupidly clever.

I write to bring value for all readers to change ideas that are misconceptions; myths or damn right lies about mental illness and our world. It's my hope that reading of my experiences will lead to greater understanding and acceptance and so help those with mental health to feel less ashamed of their disorders because there is a biological basis for them. Schizophrenia is not demonic phenomenon,

it is based in biology. Physical, social and environmental factors can also play a role in its development; the correct terminology opens up honest conversations about the disease.
I like to thank you for reading the reasons why its important for me to write, not only because it's therapeutic, but most important too is to change minds, open up understanding and connect people.

Aubrey Malone

Writing and Mental Health

I've always believed that writing, even writing about dark topics, is therapeutic. The very ability to sit down at a desk, no matter how bad we're feeling, is a victory over that mood. It's difficult to do it in today's world where everything is moving so fast. Many of us spend so much time looking into our Smartphones (which isn't too smart) or being bombarded with sound bites from billboards and television screens that we lose the still centre of ourselves. David Thoreau talked about people leading lives of "quiet desperation." Today that desperation is noisier.

My own tastes in writing veer towards the introspective. Some people synonymise that with negativity, which I think is untrue. For years, for example, people tended to think of the labyrinthine ruminations of Samuel Beckett as grim and despondent. Brendan Behan's brother Brian once described Beckett to me as "a long string of misery." It was a common perception at the time. It's only recently we've started to appreciate how hilarious a writer he was. Even if it's black comedy it's still very funny. I think Beckett used writing as a form of catharsis. The very activity of writing, the discipline it calls up and the demands it imposes, by definition rouses us from the kind of immersion in our problems that becomes the breeding ground for many forms of depression.

People had the same idea about Leonard Cohen as they had about Beckett. A snide joke going the rounds when I first started listening to this singer was that his records should be sold with razor blades in the sleeves so people could cut their wrists with them. If you take Cohen at face value, his songs do often sound morose, but I've always thought this was because his voice is so deep rather than anything endemic in the lyrics. These are often mischievous, especially in a song like "I'm Your Man", which revived his reputation back in the 1980s. I interviewed him when he was promoting it. I asked him how he felt about the razor blade comment. He said, "Once that kind of stuff gets into the computer it stays with you forever." He spent most of his life trying to convince people there was more to him than Nordic gloom. I told him I found I found his work uplifting, adding that I thought there was nothing more depressing than bad comedy. He liked that attitude.

Cohen once said, "People tell me not to complain about the rain in Canada but what else can you do when you're soaking wet?" The way we write is a response to the way we feel, and if we feel depressed we're being untrue to ourselves to go into denial about that for a kind of literature that smooth's over it, or replaces it with bromides. The longer we do this, the more it's going to haunt us. Ernest Hemingway is a good example of this. He spent most of his writing career adopting a hard-bitten dialect where he appeared impervious to the whips and scorns of time but at the end of his life all of the vulnerability he'd been suppressing with that veneer of "grace under pressure" came back with a vengeance. He ended his life by shooting himself in the head, after various bouts of electrical shock treatment failed to cure his feelings of purposelessness.

Feelings are responses to experiences. Hopefully the days are long gone when people saw depression as a weakness of character. Today, thanks to publishers like Chipmunka and many others, we're encouraged to get such feelings out of ourselves. The expression "A problem shared is a problem halved" acquires added resonance when that sharing is put down on paper. When it does, it becomes the property of the world.

Depression feeds off silence. This is something people are all too painfully aware of in Ireland, where I live, and where the rate of suicide has increased exponentially in the past few decades, especially among young men. It's a fact that men talk less about their problems than women. Go into any pub or club or restaurant or railway station or doctor's surgery or anywhere else you care to mention in any country in the world and the chances are that the men will be talking about politics or sport and the women will be sharing personal stories. It's just the way things are. Men are from Mars and women are from Venus. If there's ever life found on either of these planets, guess where the most chatting will be done?

Today, thankfully, men are starting to expose their hearts and souls on paper if not verbally, and thereby pave the way towards erasing the stereotype of the "strong silent" veneer that's dogged them for so long. With the explosion of self-publishing outlets today, and the developments in digital printing, everyone can theoretically become a writer. One of the greatest growth areas in genre publishing at the moment is in the area of self-help. You can hardly go into a bookshop today without tripping over books on the subject. What does that say to us? It says that more people than ever before are now finding it difficult to deal with their problems. The other huge growth area has been in the area of diet books.

What does this say? It says that we have a huge problem of obesity in the world. I've always thought much of the reason for this is because of comfort eating, which is a kind of by-product of depression. (In other forms of depression, of course, people under-eat).

The point to bear in mind, in any case, is that in writing we can collect around ourselves all the machinery to conquer our demons. Which isn't, of course, to suggest that it's the only way of doing so. Any form of activity is good to get us out of ourselves when we feel the world is weighing us down. Some people prefer physical forms of activity to adrenalize themselves rather than hewing words onto a page. There are no hard and fast rules for psychological stability. If there were, we could put them online and "cure" mental health problems all over the world at the touch of a computer key. But in writing we can learn what's making us unwell by digging deeper into ourselves. The Greek word "Kateban" means literally "I went down." It's a very descriptive term for the manner in which we find our inner self, a variation of the Delphic oracle "Know thyself."

Some people heal themselves by looking out instead of in. This is perhaps closer to the gospel that mindfulness preaches. But in inner meditation, be it yoga, TM or the forensic self-examination that takes place in writing, I feel we stand a better chance of – to use an expression of Kris Kristofferson's – "beating the devil.'

I published four books with Chipmunka and in the writing of each of them I found I got to know myself a little better. The first was a memoir; the other three were books of short stories. When I was a young boy at school I had trouble even writing my name. My father composed most of my school essays for me. He walked up and down the floor dictating them to me and I transcribed them. When I found I could put a few sentences together without his help it made me feel almost god-like. When my first book was published I was so excited I expected the world to almost stop spinning on its axis. It became a drug; the kind of drug alcohol had once been to me.

Writing helped me get off drink. I created worlds in my stories that were probably different versions of myself when I thought about them. I wasn't aware I was writing for any other reason than to blacken pages but as the work took on a life of its own I felt it was leading me by the hand to some obscure form of enlightenment. I rarely knew what I was going to write until I'd written it. In a sense I found myself on the page. Things that were troubling me in my subconscious came out when I wrote. It was like a dream world entering into the real one, and vice versa. Before I became a writer and something was bothering me, people used to say to me, "It won't seem as bad in the morning." They were usually right. When I wrote it down, it seemed even less bad. I was a barman in London in 1970 and I kept a dream diary. Every morning when I woke up, I wrote any dreams I had down in it. I found if I didn't do this immediately, they went clean out of my mind. Sometimes they made sense and more often they didn't seem to, but over the summer they made a mosaic that helped me realise what forms of chaos were going on inside me. You can't be afraid of a word the way you can of an unspoken thought. It's the uncertainty that creates the fear. In dreams our hidden thoughts and fears come out. They're our mind's way of protecting us from having breakdowns, its way of going to the toilet, if we can put it like that.

I'm sure I'm not the first person who ever felt their writing to be explicatory. I never expected this to happen but when it did I became almost obsessive about it. The dream diary was only a summer activity but I wrote stories right through my life. In some cases it was as if they were waiting somewhere for me to discover them, as if they had a kind of previous existence independent of me. I was grateful for them because they gave me a goal. When I started writing them I'd been drinking a lot and I knew it wasn't doing me any good. I was a teacher and my work day ended at 2.30. There was too much of the day left and I couldn't think of a productive way to spend it so, like many teachers I knew, I headed for "the high stool." I often thought of myself in the same vein as someone like George Best. Best took to drinking in almost 24-hour binges after he retired from football because he needed a high to equal the high he used to get from scoring goals and could only find it at the bottom of a glass. Other footballers, who drank too much, like Jimmy Greaves, hauled themselves back from the brink by becoming pundits – or writers.

Many of my early stories were despondent. Looking back, I think I wanted to be a part of the "angry young man" school of writing. It was only later I learned to develop a comic side to what I wrote. The writer Patrick Kavanagh once said that tragedy was undeveloped comedy. I think he had something there. Comedy and tragedy are like two sides of the one coin. If we're lucky, we learn to merge them. If we aren't, we could end up like Robin Williams, a man who played the clown for so many years he failed to understand there was a more serious man inside him trying to get out. When it did, it was in his last tragic act, the act of a Pagliacci, as he hanged himself. Maybe if Williams had committed his thoughts to paper instead of camouflaging them in his incredible range of personas, he would still be with us today.

Louise Hart

Manifesto for a Dream
By
Louise M. Hart

In the 1970's I sit at a writing desk, my classmates surround me. The teacher hands me a photocopied photograph. She asks the class to write a story inspired by the picture. I look at the image and in a flash decide to write about the creation of a flying machine and the inventor who produces it. Professor P. Nut is born. I am lost in a textual haven of words and images that fuel my imagination, like the TV cartoons I watch when I return home from school. I am lost and then, I am found.

My teacher read my completed story to the class. Sometime in those few minutes, I experienced my first moment of being, the precipice of a second in which I realized that my destiny existed as a priori as the existence of language. I was fated not to be a hairdresser or teacher, a nurse or a scientist, but a writer. In the throes of my realization, life became worthwhile. When she read my story aloud, my teacher had legitimated me and writing birthed my identity, as surely as my Mother had produced my physical form.

It is 2018 I stand onstage in a Birmingham pub. In my hands are 3 poems typed on paper. My hands shake with nervous anticipation. I begin to read them aloud before an audience of members and supporters of a charitable organisation. I have read my poems at public events many times before, but each time fear remains my unwanted companion. Fear of not representing my work to its full efficacy. But, fear is a false adversary. Like the neighbour who smiles when she faces you, but gossips about you when you are out of sight, it encumbers your experiential status at only the most superficial level. After all, no matter how ineptly I read my work, I, and only I, wrote it. Reading is interpretation, writing is the thing-in-itself.

Goodbye sweet soul
I loved you well
But, now, your presence
Honours hell
Where morning breaks
Amidst the glow
Of sacred Mothers

Suckling foe
There lies an essence
Of a smile
Washed ashore
On a golden mile
Of sand encrusted
Smiles and shells
Whose destination
No one knows
Some say
It clings to life
Like a thorn
To a blood red rose
Then pricks the heart
Of pain's repose

The poem above became my first published piece. It was a simple and alliterative poem that featured in a poetry anthology in 2011. But, when I saw it printed in a book, featuring my name beneath it, I swelled with pride. The experience was analogous to my teacher reading my story at school. But, there were not 10 years between the experiences, as I had anticipated, but over 30.

Life had thwarted my noble ambition; the linear reality between the then and now moments when experience had marked me with blows so devastating that I would be thrust in the litter bin of non-achievement. Life had been cruel; I had developed mental health issues, but I continued to cling to it, like my sanity. Thus, central to my writing manifesto is a recovery narrative.

C. Jess-Cooke in their paper, Rethinking Creative Writing Pedagogy for Recovery from Mental Illness (2015), argues, "Creative writing that is not used as an intervention for mental illness can profit from engagement with therapeutic approaches." Whilst there is a plethora of research on the therapeutic properties of expressive writing, creative writing has been underexplored. I would argue that this is attributable to the crude and reductionist manner in which academia often perceives the, "mad subject," or those affected by mental health issues.

I am every colour of the rainbow
And many shades…

Creative writing demands that a writer reaches beyond the confines of the, "I;" she must explore other landscapes and consciousness's. Expressive writing centralises subjectivity, rendering self both form and subject of a written piece. Thus, the mad writer who subjugates herself in creative prose has vanquished the implied and connoted rule of expressive writing that madness cannot perceive beyond itself. This rule should be smashed, broken, like the purpose of a series of commas in a rambling sentence.
...In between

If my psychosis were a colour
It would be purple

When I wrote my first published novel, I attempted to ameliorate the rule. Although it was a novel, it conformed to the conventions of mad writing and embraced a style that challenged traditional novel writing and language that was hyper-real and expressive in nature. In Writing and Madness, Shoshana Felman argues that madness not only teaches us about literature but constitutes it. For her, madness represents, "an irreducible resistance to interpretation."

Joy and misery define life
But purple defines me

Felman claims that the mad text is neither signified or signifier, but it is a rhythm. Thus, my writing expresses the chords of my consciousness, the textual music of a mind that negates its madness, only to reinforce it many fold. I write to resist both the restrictions of the physical realm that binds me and ideological control. Like my work, I am irreducible and traditional theorization struggles to interpret me. We are what we write.
The image of Charlotte Perkins Gilman writing The Yellow Wallpaper to save her sanity haunts me and symbolizes the plight of many struggling writers, fighting to affirm their talent beneath the weight of minds, almost too heavy to bear. Since writing my first and inevitably autobiographically inspired novel, I have embraced the wonders of gothic and

weird fiction. These genres, favoured by writers, like Perkins Gilman, Poe and Machen, are often associated with explorations of the nature of madness/sanity and have offered me a textual stage on which to perform my words and encode my ideas. Moreover, whilst writing is a serious business, gothic fiction permits an element of fun, which heightens my enjoyment of the creative process and is thereby reflected in the work I produce.

Foucault argues that medicine and psychiatry do not allow us to understand mental health, thus we must engage with writing by mad writers, like Nietzsche and Artaud to comprehend its nature. This view can be extended beyond mental health. Writing reveals more about the writer than a conversation and even a therapy session can do. For a text encodes the consciousness of a writer and clues to her subconscious and unconscious identities.

I sit in a warm and comfortable house, typing on a laptop that I own. I am not Virginia Woolf's, Judith Shakespeare, Shakespeare's fictional sister, whom she imagined in her seminal text, A Room of one's Own. I am a woman of the twenty-first century, with a room of my own and an income and lifestyle independent of men. When I write, I reflect the material conditions of both my life and the epoch in which I live. The socio-political and ideological circumstances of my existence present in my words; my writing is an instruction manual of the superstructure of British life in 2018 and my position in the manual a reflection of my relation to the infrastructure of the society and country in which I live.

Whilst my gender does not determine my writing, I am acutely aware of how it affects it. Woolf argues that the best writers possess androgynous minds. I aspire to achieve this in every piece I write. However, I am a woman living in a patriarchal society, where men's writing is frequently valued above that of women. Undeniably, this influences the subjects of and themes about which I choose to write. However, I do not believe that gender dictates the nature and form of my writing.

Arguably, Woolf created a woman's sentence. The circularity of her prose and her perception of time differ from that present in the form and structure of traditional male writing, which employs a more linear literary model. Hitherto, many female writers have attempted to replicate the women's sentence. I, too, have consciously eschewed the constraints of traditional male narratives, but would argue that this emanates not from my essential womanhood, but it is wholly aesthetic. The women's sentence and mine, also, constitute, thus, a symbolic rebellion against patriarchy. They signify our disparate society, not gender.

Without an examination of the impact of writing on one's cognition, emotions and spiritual being, a contemplation of the creative process would be incomplete. Whilst it yields deconstructing, the act of putting ink to paper is transcendent. When I write I become an, "other," external to myself and perhaps, bigger and grander. I am not merely the guardian of my pen, but a conduit through which speaks the voice of truth; the truth is inspiration and she resides somewhere between the tip of my pen and the periphery of my mind.

I write then, I die a little, becoming a willowy Chatterton-like figure, clinging to my poison chalice of words. But, unlike Chatterton, when I consume poison, I create words and am reborn, each time in slightly different skin.

I write
Usually, at night
To feel better

Writing has not cured my mental distress, but it has made me feel insurmountably better. It is comparable to experiencing a rush of blood to the head. The moment of creation is like an orgiastic second in which all the problems of the universe dissolve, clarity is discovered and utopia realized. Whilst this feeling is only transitory, its effects linger. Writing as an act of creation changes one's heart, mind and soul irrevocably.

Catharsis through writing has become clichéd, the property of memoir writing celebrities and self-help gurus. But, the reality is that it can facilitate the transformation of the architecture of one's psychical being. Before I wrote with any degree of seriousness, my demeanor was both externally and inwardly more negative. My creative process has helped rewire my cerebral circuitry in a way that has benefitted me and the world around me. The act of creation not only elevates mood, but challenges one's notions about one's ontological and existential identity.

As a human being I constitute the summation of every text I have ever read and, in turn, every piece of writing I produce regurgitates those texts. Thus, I am uniquely unoriginal and my writing is thinly veiled plagiarism, masquerading as original prose and poetry. However, I own both the process by which I write and its product.

When words arrive in my mind, they shine, like gifts from a force that is beyond my somatic being and intellect. Were I religious, I would thank higher beings for presenting them to me. But, in reality, words emanate from within my consciousness. Their apparent otherworldliness is a trick, played by the trajectory of inspiration and I merely am a product of the self-textualised pen of consensual reality.

As I started, so I shall end.

I sit at a table
I am NOTHING
I write
I am everything

Kundera knew
He saw the lack
His writing
Sealed a gap

A gaping whole
In every soul
That bled
NOTHING

Unbearably light
He wrote
Everything
From NOTHING

I am not
Of his kind
A genius of words
And mind

But, like him
I write everything
From
NOTHING

Andrew Cheffings,

Bits of Hope

When I write, I am my own audience. I see the words form, the sentences grow before me on this sheet of paper, and think of forests and workers and machines and ships and lorries and oil fields and labourers lost at sea, and I don't want to waste a valuable line or a precious page.

    I speak these lines and make the air vibrate with my voice. Some listen, some rush past, eyes down, and some grumble, hunched over, beneath their breath, while still others walk tall, smile like lighthouses and throw a few coins out my way from time to time.   Maybe I once dreamed of openings and glowing Guardian reviews, interviews on the local news and late at night on BBC2, but now I am mostly my own listener. I tell myself stories, sometimes to entertain, but more often to warn and make myself pay attention to voices I have tried to lock away in inner, hidden rooms, bereft of sunlight, wreathed in gloom.

         He sits, deep in that rough-hewn pit, a tiny opening, high above, projecting weak rays of greenish sunlight onto rocky projections, just out of reach, on which, self-bonsai-ed saplings barely find a place to wither. But, looking up, he sees forests bathed in golden light there, where distant happy beings softly tread across thick leaf-mould among the gentle creatures of the woodland floor.
         And, as I drag the words from this cheap but costly pen, I can transfer the prisoner from his rock-bound prison to those leafy glades, for neither he nor they have any substance beyond my mind and both can be transmuted if I choose carefully my similes and metaphors.

         Then, while he walks free there, eating delicious sun-ripened berries from the woodland edge, other, hidden beings watch on in ever-growing alarm, for their peace of mind depends, they think, on keeping him crushed down, silenced and out-of-sight.   So, now I have to deal with them as well, and give them other metaphors and myths to chew on, places other than watch-towers to live in. I write them gardens, made safe from the world of cruel words – which cut and burn – with house-high hedges circling out all that's beyond, situated on mountain tops, high above the clouds, which hide the forest, far below, beneath their vaporous, droplet-laden banks.

Sometimes, all that's needed is to separate my warring parts and keep them occupied and entertained with labyrinthine, metaphoric narratives, send them on adventures, epic journeys and mystic quests, giving me the time to meditate and merge my whole world within with the formless, universal life-force.

Other times, I feel I need to give them names and characters and histories and karmas, and write them out of conflict into creative co-operation or at least, grudging co-existence. I write a united nations of my subconscious mind to work through conflict, and make a bill of universal rights, and work towards an inner world in which all voices are listened to and heard and made to feel supported and part of something larger than their isolated-seeming selves.

If I could but achieve this with these black marks on this page, before it starts noticeably to yellow, I might achieve some peace of mind for myself, and little bits of hope and inspiration for any suffering beings with whom they chime and resonate.

Is Writing Cathartic

A Personal Take On The Topic in Mental Health: by Anne Brocklesby

I have five published books with *Chipmunka Publishing* – yes I do like that catchy name - which I would say were probably cathartic writings, all completed in a few short years. The first three just came out of my head, as I sat at the computer, and the words tumbled out, page after page about emotions, about life, about feelings, about not coping, and having a complete and utter breakdown. Now that was cathartic in the sense that these ideas were just going round and round my head, and a whole load of poems which cleverly formulated their lines in my sleep, both unconsciously and then subconsciously, and remained there until I wrote them down. It helped empty my head. It is an incredible feat in a way, being able to just write poems, and condense everything into a poem instead of a book, because poems can be so expressive. I had an unusual friend who wrote poetry and music and tried to deal with her explosive history in that creative way.

Sometimes words to poems are empathic – because if we 'know' what someone else is going through, we can identify with them, and maybe we can put into words what they are struggling with. It is a great gift to intuitively be able to relate to another human being on that higher plane involving our amazing senses, and also help them understand why those feelings arose in the first place. It can be cathartic to write, and also to be read, so readers pay attention too. I mean, "Does anybody care out there?" Perhaps that is the title of someone's new book.

Writing is an art, just as playing music, or performing theatrical drama, or getting creative in the kitchen is too. One very successful piece of writing I did was a paper on the development of the arts in schools – a fun piece to write, and to read, or read back, and reflect on. Some fifty years later I still remember that informative and authoritative writing – it had grabbed my attention and I just felt compelled to write. I passed that exam with flying colours.

I have always enjoyed real life situations more than fictional ones. I find that the idea of fantasy can be dangerous, you might want to slip into that other role, you might feel envious, or indeed somehow seek out friendships or activities, which are not inherently good for you. In my early childhood we always chose both factual and fictional books at the library visit, still prescribed for a good balance in life. We could learn facts and expand our rote and factual learning, but we could also read interesting stories. My favourite books were little gang ones, like Famous Five and Secret Seven by Enid Blyton. I felt I could belong, with others, in exciting situations; it was almost like imaginary friends. I once had a real life gang – gang of five, to include my two younger sisters and two other girls and we would meet up in the shed in our garden. I also liked Noddy books, as Toytown had much going on for everyone, and he had a friend called Big Ears. As a teenager I enjoyed historical novels, like Jean Plaidy and Anya Seyton, which I read avidly, alongside poetry, which prompted me to write down my own ideas. I liked sad books like Thomas Hardy's – I could imagine myself in some of those situations because his descriptions were so real – and explorer adventure stories, both factual and fictional, where brave people were pioneers in their travels or chosen fields of work.

I won many books as prizes at school, and always worked hard academically, and one really awful book I received was about torture of political prisoners. I always believed in fair play, and a just society, and this carried on into my later work, when I became a qualified social worker. School was structured, fair and firm, and we had plenty of cultural activities, music appreciation, singing, drama, social activities, plus compulsory team sport, so I became quite good at netball, and a good goal shooter. I also liked to enjoy myself too, to go out with friends, to cinema, dancing, drama group and our local ice rink, the meet up place.

So, returning to writing as catharsis, as a topic mind, I most liked the last two books I wrote: one about our senses, and the need to be aware of them and to use and follow them, and the one about holding on to our mental health and how we need to prevent mental distress. Life has its ups and downs - Life Happens, or try Life Happens Anyway. The Arts Council England sponsored my book **'Let's Hang On To Mental Health – Why We Need To Prevent Mental Distress'** and I was justifiably proud of that, seeing their endorsement on the cover. Both books involved committed research, some undertaken specifically to write the book, and other research prompted by my campaigning work in the field of mental health. Not many people spoke up about the topic of mental health, and how it felt as an end user; to be dealt with in the complicated hit and miss system of health and social care. When we survey the destructive scene some years later, yes things have improved, because it is now reasonably OK to speak publicly about mental health when someone chooses to do that, for others to write about their experiences, or for some to portray their feelings through art, music, comedy or drama.

But, and that is a big but, our world is global, with many diverse and international issues to deal with, as well as cope with local dilemmas of financial cuts resulting in fewer services, and our society could be viewed as fragmentary. But, when you look around, you find that there are many positive approaches in community development, little pockets of people helping others, and initiatives which are gradually changing dysfunctional structures and out-dated services. Mental Health publishing has its place in that.

Throughout my working life, outside the family, I helped run a number of different local charities and offered general help, advice and support to people who came through the door, or were there when we did outreach work, which is an essential part of any professional's approach to work. And voluntary work, getting involved in varied groups in the community, like the parents association at our children's' schools, where we were all struggling to help our children grow into happy and responsible adults, and helping other children to read and write as I had helped my own, by volunteering time in schools. Sharing in person, or in writing, or other artistic means, helps others learn, and the sharer can feel better for it, maybe by unloading or hearing reflected comments and feedback.

My most recent paid works were in the field of mental health. One in the voluntary sector, a voice for people who were affected by the mental health system, and lack of services, and reflecting views back to the authority responsible for providing both inpatient and outpatient health and social care. In fact, on reflection, it was a very crucial central role, being able to accurately pick up on what people, both users and carers, were actually saying, or had written, rather than just 'listening' with deaf ears. I needed to collate and put that information forward verbally and in writing, to salary earners who were able to make changes and improve services. That was a very taxing job. And the second paid job, was one of those zero hours jobs, where you go in as an experienced user of mental health services and are supposed to work, on equal terms for a pittance, with paid professional salaried staff in the health and social care sector, where the role is to support current service users, try to advocate and just be there for them. I found that 'job' impossible, mainly due to the lack of respect from some professional staff and the impossibility of providing anything like the kind of support which the individual service users needed, due to the lack of resources in the health and social care sector. Far better for such peer support services to be run on a voluntary basis I think. That was reflected in my volunteer work for the local Mind group where I helped establish their Newsletter, another written medium, as I had done in my work earlier with the then Area Health Authority.

Campaigning work can be cathartic, and for balance relaxation. For fun, I like music, I enjoy the theatre, watching films, and creative courses like willow weaving, vegetarian cookery, art in landscape and still life, drama, barge painting, Japanese gardens, gardening, aquaerobics, meditation, etc. Sometimes though we need a bit of a rest, and it can be peaceful, and sustaining, to spend time quietly reflecting and re-learning how *to be*. And for me these quieter times can involve writing and poetry.

I find it helpful to have that time on my own. I like to think, but not overthink. I like to write to clear my head of ideas, and also sometimes I can write to order, for example if I wanted to write a poem as a contribution for a poetry book, or indeed contributing this short piece for Chipmunka for the **Anthology on Mental Health Writing As Catharsis**. Somebody once gave me an idea for an art/poetry session - "I'm A Nobody, Who Are You? Emily Dickinson wrote that famous poem – good on her. Who are we anyway? I liked the way that the poem pulled me in. I mean, who Am I? And as Eric Berne wrote in his book, "What Do You Say After You Say Hello?"

At senior school, our headmistress asked us to write about 'Who Am I?' I seem to remember enjoying the topic, and attempting the task, but not really sure who I was. I remember writing something like I would see how it all worked out – I was about 17 years of age at the time. Yes, it was a religious based school, but no, my essay did not have to be about religion, or beliefs. I was free to write about who I was. The only difficulty being, I did not really know. So I think that writing helps me explore a topic, it helps me focus and concentrate on the issue at hand, rather than go off in too many directions at once, or on tangents. It is good for our mental health!

I try to be a realist. To try and appreciate life for what it really is. Sometimes hard to bear, and other times quite fun. I like to enjoy myself. Through hard tough times I have also tried hard to be true to myself. Someone once wrote to me, if you are an apple, then do not try and become a pear. And who am I? I like to think that I am an honest person, solid to the core, and incredibly patient. I come up against temptation and trials like everyone else, but, eventually can rise to the challenge, face it, and try and help other people along the way too.

I used to think I was an optimist, but that is a falsehood in reality. Nothing ever always goes right, just like nothing always goes wrong. I am learning now, even by writing this article, which I am enjoying. I am searching, exploring, and discovering new things and ideas, evolving, moving on, into learning to be the best that I can be. I do not hold the philosophy that we are just what we are. That is like the old Popeye cartoon, "I am what I am - I am Popeye the Sailor Man". He ate his spinach, and yes that is good for you, but somehow he turned into a superman. I am not a superhero, but just like everyone else, doing the best that I can.

It is sometimes hard to continue to move on and thrive, when we are held back by this constantly busy society or when we maybe get stuck in a groove; but hey, maybe I like the old track, which continues to play. So I stick around, and I try to learn to groove too, and learn how to dance to a new theme or tune even. So *catharsis* implies release. From what? And onto where? I would say that writing can support release, in a constructive way, by helping me for example, to explore ideas, which just spill out, or which are more consciously formed prior to delivery. For example, I thought about this catharsis topic for about two weeks before putting anything down on paper. So writing can be haphazard, or just random, or more structured, but there must be some sort of logic to it too.

There are many styles of writing, and another form of mental health writing is creative writing. I attended a mental health creative writing group for a number of years, and found I mainly wrote in a 'stream of consciousness' kind of way, as did Virginia Woolf too. That was my style – letting it cascade out, whatever the topic was. Nowadays I find I try to write with a more ordered approach. It helps me organise my mind, to bring it all back in together. It is more like writing a report. I can also do a mind mapping approach to writing, where I try and create threads, and then do my best to weave them together, somehow, by elaboration, then summarising, so I can come to some sort of conclusion, or maybe point the way for further investigation and research. When I have something written down on the page - usually typed in my case, although I know some people like to write pen to paper, and I can do that too - I can feel justifiably proud of myself. I have been creative, produced something, which I hope others will read. Occasionally I also write just for myself – and that is more the darker recesses or troubles I may be thinking I am experiencing, more like the flashback which imposes itself on my mind. Distraction is a good technique there, afterwards, when the writing is finished, and what do I do with the writing? Sometimes I just throw it away or delete it, as I fundamentally know that it is rubbish, and that my life has moved on from the past. But I need to express it, because I was not able to do so at the time.

I have also helped run a couple of mental health poetry sessions in community groups, and also on psychiatric wards. Sometimes I would read a poem out, and bring along a book which also had illustrations, as it can sometimes be the words, and other times the pictures which sparks enthusiasm for writing, or for being creative on the piece of paper. Some of the most effective words on paper can be maybe just a short sentence, or even disjointed words. Not a long rambling piece. That reminds me of the wonderful R D Laing piece on *'Knots'*. What goes around, comes around is a useful approach to remember. By sharing our knowledge and experiences we can help others, just as we too have been helped. I was lucky, because one of my grandfathers had been a headmaster, and he taught me to read and write before I even went to school. I have always been able to read, or write, or both. Sometimes though it has been more difficult to speak out. I have always been able to listen, and be an active listener, so that has helped me. And for some of us, using the medium of writing in difficult situations can be an easier way of communicating and communing with others, as opposed to speaking out or speaking up, at least sometimes.

Returning to the topic of writing - poetry and art, or pictures - one of the more recent group activities I took part in was exploring creating art work, inspired by poems, either ones we had written ourselves, or ones we brought in from a book. If you think of writing, it can be very pictorial, think of eastern languages and their symbols. The short course, of four sessions was followed up by a poetry recital where the participants had one art work displayed on the gallery wall, and also could read out two of their own poems. I now have some of my own artwork at home on the wall. One piece I really like – it is colourful spices in a Moroccan market as seen from above – so many bright colours, like a scattered rainbow. I will keep that one, but the others, no. I hope you have found this article informative and descriptive, as well as illustrating the art of cathartic writing styles.

And to finish, an example of a short form of writing – a poem I wrote some years ago: -

That Wretched Nettle - a poem by Anne Brocklesby

That wretched nettle stung me
It pricked my finger tip
As I was tidying up the earth
Below the olive tree
It opened up its jaws
And made some sword like cuts
It hurt, it really stung me
Through the tip to the finger, the hand and the arm
I started to shake
Paralysis of body next and the Internet said it could eventually lead to death

HELP

John Welsh

Jason's anthology

The Write thing to do

There is laundry to be sorted
Pots around the sink
The fridge is showing empty
But my heart says pen and ink

Carpets needing a hoover
Rubbish to be taken out
Though I see a story starting
But what to write about

All seem like urgent distractions
You only have to look
However top of my list of chores
Is to sit down and write a book

Maybe I should get a maid in
A servant to free my time
But I need a few bestsellers
Before that dream is mine

John the local poet

How writing lifts my mood!

By John Welsh 2018
lists

I love lists! The first line on a new list should be make a list.
There is a sense of extreme satisfaction in completing or small part transferring and then binning a list.
Whether just to do lists, shopping, memory joggers or wish the worktops, fridge door or even electronic reminders in my world my lists ebb and flow like the tides
Master list's with post it attachments could be a new art form.

Journals

I write mine at going to bed time and try to write the thoughts of the day rather than just list the actions (that would seem like a back list)
It's a bit like the defragmentation of my mind before some sleep and loses some of the clutter that could easily be a distraction in the tumble dryer of bipolar thinking.

Fast poetry to go

Triggers that start a poem can come at any moment.
Overheard words and phrases, glimpsed visions, sensed even smelt can start the process.
I write very quickly once triggered, often within seconds and usually write the complete poem with no break or edit. If the trigger comes as a middle of the night reflection then I grab the always handy pen and paper and get it down in its pure fresh to thought form.

Story writing/telling

Like some bipolar creative writers I am vocal and my mind tends to go off on tangents away from a thought track. This is where the weaving comes into play especially when progressing an often complex plot.
Take people, put them in places at certain times and create situations.
Add more people, link in remote places sometimes crossing different continents and centuries and then combine all the above.

This is multilevel fiction and I imagine to some readers (not the author) these can be confusing like chasing a mole down a dark passage.

I know where I am going from the forewords and page 1 and can visualise the action and as I said before I just have to weave and add in extra flourishes as I go.

I write for myself primarily in this genre and recognise an autobiographical thread which is I think expected and make my own books and sell them in my own style which I have adopted (a book in a box) which again ticks my creative ego Neither King nor Pharaoh, hero or saviour, villain or shady character I just include some traits of my condition like extreme emotion and escapism.

These stories may be brilliant or truly awful
If I decide to publish them wider I will have to adapt them into a more recognisable style.

Performance

I am a poet with bipolar!

I do not have any issue with being marginalised.

Poetry seemed to choose me back in 1969

I can be funny, sad and thoughtful and I regularly go on stage and attend writing workshops where I can give my audience a brief insight into what they are about to hear.

The performing bug has bitten me like the writing bug. Because of it often being of a very personal nature I very rarely buy other poets work although I have an extensive bookcase of mixed work

I have talked about triggers and one example I repeat is a true tale about a female friend who was having a chat with and her phone rang. She moved away but stayed within earshot and said to the caller " No I am sorry I can't as I am having a cat flap fitted"

Now that's a trigger and I wrote a poem called "The reason's I can't"

I do not worry about losing my physical health but have some concerns as I move into old age about losing my memory which I feel is pretty good especially long term. Germination of an idea can take quite a long time. The longest seed to sprout was 40 years. I have travelled regularly up to the North West and crossed over the moors From North Yorkshire to Cumbria.

The language on the sign posts changes in that very rural rugged region and I remember seeing a way sign with "Scarcrag cottage" on it although I could not see the building. For a long time I wondered if there was honeysuckle over the lintel and Fuchsia in hanging baskets I never found out but I wrote "My love is like a bloom on the crag"
With that in mind.
Its on page 35 of my first book of life poems
Manic Reflections published by Chipmunka
Another area I have explored and this again is where my long memory comes in is fusing together two or more ideas. Often in my early life in Sheffield I would sit with friends in bars and we would tell jokes (often long story jokes) I have a good recall of these and for the last couple of years I have given these stories a new lease of life and produced a compilation of 16 as poems which I call Com-etry.
They make me laugh even though a lot of them originate from a slightly non-pc era of the 70's. I know I can be rude but never crude
As I said I do not edit however some poems I have returned to and extended because I felt I had something more to say.
Writing is I believe a true therapy

Andrew Voyce MA

I see the main aspects of personal narrative and mental health as:
*It's therapeutic activity in a therapeutic space
*It's a cathartic activity in that it may cleanse difficult experiences and enable moving on
*It gives you something tangible - a book, song, poem or game - to share with others, be they friends, family, or caregivers
*It gives you something of your experience in your terms, your pictures and words, your voice: not someone else's version of who you are

I've gained by writing and drawing my experience, in that I was able to detail and quantify my episodes of psychosis, and to recognise what it was and to help me move on. The manager of the day centre back then said to me: you couldn't have done this a few years ago, could you? And she was right, I couldn't then have recognised my experience as a system of delusion and paranoia.

I've been able to share my story with all sorts of people, and especially with my family where it has helped me to reconnect with relatives, and those who have good connections with family will know that. I can give talks and people will go away with one of my books to help them help others with mental health challenges.

I can listen to other people's stories and make their narratives come to life with the cathartic outcome that I have had.'

Rehana Incognito. "Bodycage"

The first thought which comes to mind in regard to writing one's own story, whether autobiography or fictional story alluding to our own, is the fact that we survived to tell it! Then, having survived and finding ourselves still with the capability to put our thoughts together, we can write it all out to not only process everything that happened in our lives, but use the experience to educate and help others.

This is exactly where I found myself when Jason Pegler contacted me personally, after the incredible "coincidence" of watching him on a TV interview and thinking to myself how much I would love to meet him. Within a couple of days of thinking just that, I had. So followed the inspirational guidance to write out the story of my particular journey and published the novel "Bodycage" through Chipmunka Publishing.

It's definitely true that starting from the beginning of earliest things we can remember and processing through our now adult perspective, is very cathartic. Step by step we can look at incidences and events in our lives (many of which had caused us extreme harm and distress, affecting our development and outlook along the way!) from an almost objective perspective. From my own adult perspective, I was able to look at myself as "the child" who had no way to really process harmful behaviours which came my way from other people, especially adults and these harms and injustices simply became part of who I became or was.

In looking at "the child", I spent moments along the way to actually speak to the childhood self and offer comfort from all I have learned since, seeing the behaviour of others had everything to do with their own messed up thinking and beliefs... and little to do with who this child was. In looking at these events, it became easier to see how the mistakes of others had caused me to adapt my own behaviour and personality, no longer blaming myself and finding fault. So many of the "mistakes" we then go on to make in our own lives, which harmed us or others, can then be seen for what they are- attempts to mask or hide, subdue or lash out at things we could not process or take on board... and were not true!

Then it became easier to see that "their" wrongs were not my fault... and psychologically "replace" this damage with what I know is healthy and true for all of us.. Right now.   In understanding more about this forgiving process (giving something FOR the wrong doing), writing about it helped me realise that these events, which shaped who I am, actually shaped a better person who knew what it meant to be very caring and protective of others. Falling into old patterns, which really no longer served me, nor others, became no longer attractive or an operating system I was on.

In summary, I'd say (and recommend) writing everything out and looking deeply into all the experiences and events, which shaped us.   In trying to find a way to understand how we've reacted and absorbed negative or abusive incidents, find a way to learn something of benefit (forgive) from past events... and let it all go and be grateful for the better people we are because of it, not in spite of it.   With this understanding comes much self-love, and even forgiveness of ourselves, forever thinking that messed up people had ever been right! Then we can move on and be free to enjoy a better life and create much better situations for ourselves and others.

Much love and best wishes to whoever reads this.

Barbara Goulden

Writing down your thoughts is a great release - a bit like yoga only on a keyboard.
I was aged 11 when my sister became mentally ill. I didn't understand it, not did my baffled parents. We only knew that she'd become obsessed with a church minister who'd moved away from the parish he served meaning she would no longer see him.
She was only twenty-one and couldn't accept he had gone. Dangerously, she began to jump off buses believing he was travelling in a car behind her.
She was persuaded to go to the doctor's and then to the hospital. But nobody told my parents she was having a schizophrenic episode. And certainly not one that would last, on and off, for the next 50 years.
For me she was the sister who introduced me to classical music, took me to see interesting films - provided I washed my face first - and generally raised my expectations of life and its possibilities.
In writing about her, I wanted to say how all the doctors in the world had not been as supportive as the friends she made while living in sheltered housing following several terrifying electric shock treatments. The charity that manages the accommodation today is called Making Space.
It was equally important for me to explain to people who fear mental illness that delusional conditions like schizophrenia - which in severe cases can indeed be fearful - can also be lived with and even laughed at times.
I turned my sister's personal journey through madness into a novel - a humorous novel in a bid to dispel some of the stigma associated with the schizophrenia and to try to explain how a person can believe something completely outlandish on one level and be utterly rational and sane in other aspects of their life.
In the end and thanks to Chipmunka it was two novels: Knock Knock, Who's There? And Knocking On Haven's Door.
It seemed to me that if partners and family members can see delusions for what they are - misfiring brain cells - then they can perhaps accept the rest of their loved one's personality and bolster the sane. If only I'd done that instead of shouting

about my sister's irrational beliefs as I so often, and so uselessly did.

Everything fell into place for me when a friend - who'd had some training as a psychiatric nurse - was able to look in hospital records and illicitly tell me the doctors had diagnosed schizophrenia.

I still don't believe my parents ever knew. It was a long time ago and no doubt the psychiatrists of the 1950s and early 1960s thought they were protecting us from such a terrible diagnosis.

But if we'd known, we might have understood and been able to help, instead of hinder potential rehabilitation. As it happened, fellow ex-patients were able to do so much more than we could.

Writing about the experience of being mentally ill, or being close to somebody suffering from a psychosis or depression, is the only way to raise awareness.

I'm glad to see more is being done today, including finally by the army for traumatised ex-soldiers whose condition can be triggered by seeing such terrible things on the battlefield. Hopefully they will also write about their feelings. Hopefully, organisations like Chipmunka will be around to put their thoughts into print and give them - and all other sufferers of mental illness - some form of cathartic closure.

About Personal Narrative
by Andrew Voyce MA

It was shortly after the advent of community care in the early 1990's that I was encouraged to write down the things that had preoccupied me during five years of psychosis spent living in bus shelters, which ended in 1991. The manager of the day centre said to me: You couldn't have written this a few years ago, could you? And she was right – I could not have done that.

So what is it I find helpful about telling my story? There are four aspects: it is a therapeutic moment to take time to write those things; it is cathartic in that it allows you to identify and move on from those times; you have a personal document in the shape of a book to share with others, be they family, friends or caregivers; and possibly most important is that you can regain a sense of self, you can re-establish an identity. Therefore, telling my story in book and cartoon form has helped me to make sense of many lost years, years lost to psychosis, the mental health system, and homelessness.

Andrew Voyce MA December 2018

Zekria Ibrahimi

VERSE AS CATHARSIS- OR CRISIS?

Catharsis- a discharge and a relief,
Inevitably transitory and brief?
Now I am staring at a 'hp' screen,
With a keyboard, and a 'mouse' in between...
I think about *madness*, and I am old-
Sixty, almost- and does the mind grow cold,
Freeze, so that all of youth's cruel crazy heat
Becomes irrelevant, with time's harsh beat,
With the years and their always callous tread?
Madness is a fire, of desire- and dread.

This Word Processor has circuits that buzz,
While what is my mind but just fuss and fuzz?
It boasts a steel casing, looks robotic,
While I am fidgeting and half-neurotic,
Elderly, unfocussed, pathetic junk...

I think back to the seventies, when PUNK
Shouted out rebellion, boiling, wild-
Nothing about PUNK was gentle and mild-
I was a teenager, looked fresh and clean,
While Radio One had banned Johnny Rotten...
Should the *madness* of the past be forgotten,
Or, rather, maybe weirdly, celebrated?
A tension must be in me, unabated...

That tension is the fact of being sixty,
A matter of shame, teasing, taunting, tricksy,
Which I- so powerless- cannot amend.
Time is, we all discover, not a friend.

The screen, in front of me, is a cruel eye,
Condemning all that I am as a lie.
The keyboard, where I attempt to write truth,
Must know I have no substance, have no proof
That I am anything but a false freak.
Honesty is what the writer should seek.
The mouse, which I have to shift here and there,

Surely contains cybernetic despair...

Interrogated by my own computer,
By RAM, ROM, and also the wifi router,
I find out I am flesh, instead of steel,
Fragile and weak, falling apart piecemeal.

Madness is just the kingdom of delusion,
Where a mind is fixed on such fake confusion,
Madness is an iceberg, gleaming and cruel,
In which life is trapped, *madness*, like a ghoul,
Haunts me, sectioned, medicated, afraid.
Is *madness* a cage? Is it being free?
How much is it a curse of pain on me?

PUNK, it was condemned as sick and insane-
And I hear the Sex Pistols shriek again,
Against the Queen and the fascist regime,
Not on loudspeakers, but, instead, in dream.

PUNK was catharsis, releasing our fury,
PUNK told us that power was not judge and jury,
That we could make freedom instead our law,
And PUNK rebelled, it shouted more and more,
And it seemed valid, unlike priests and police,
Magistrates, M.P.s, stating, without cease,
That hearts must be repressed, repressed, repressed...
I nod off, in my armchair, frail, at best...

I am grey, wrinkled, dismally arthritic.
Time, always the snide and underhand critic,
Soon mocks the young, since they, of course, will age.
Did we then, amidst PUNK and its pure rage,
Imagine we would be pensioners? No.
I crawl round my flat, scarcely 'on the go',
Await my social worker, and I muse,
How time, that tyrant, ensures we shall lose
Dignity, self-respect, the force of love.
I switch off, with an old man's clumsy shove,
The computer, having made its screen rhyme-
Not elegantly- I am not sublime-
I am simply a creature of pretence.

Catharsis maybe seems the core of sense.

ZEKRIA IBRAHIMI (AGED 59)

Erica Loberg

POEM: ZERO

Without my writing
What do I have?

Zero means to handle reality
Zero means to breathe
Zero means to survive

Zero Zero Zero.

Sounds extreme, but it's the truth. Writing is everything to me. Writing is my best friend, my boyfriend, and my creator. It is also my Achilles heel, my destroyer, and at times my worst enemy. It has given me freedom and a platform to communicate my thoughts, but it has also imprisoned me.

Often times people ask me about my writing process and truthfully, I don't have one. Well, not in a conventional sense where I sit down at a blank screen and say, "I'm going to write today!" I've never done that cause I don't initial the writing process. Writing has always come to me. I can be on the train, and see a child swinging her feet up and down, and witness how it affects the people around her, and write a poem about my observation. Or, I am at a drag queen bar, and use the bathroom and there are strobe lights rotating around and start writing a poem on a napkin about the wild scene. I can experience an intense feeling, and have the urgency to capture that emotion in a swift moment and immediately pen a poem. So as you can see, it comes to me. I've never felt in control of my writing, and I don't do anything to initiate the process on my own which I consider to be a gift.

When it comes to content, I've never had a mind that could make things up. I'm not creative like that but, I find my life to be somewhat interesting so thankfully, I've always had material at my fingertips. When I experience something, or feel something passionately inside, I am overcome with the need to write it down which I guess is a form of release or "cathartic" but, writing is more than that to me. I never know when the carnal desire to write takes hold or will hit. I could be out and about or sitting home silent, and it takes over my being. It can be exhausting, and having a hypomanic condition has never made it any easier. But I'm not complaining.

A colleague at work recently made a joke that my books are my babies since I don't have kids, and she's right. I'd say 30 percent of my writing is about the process of writing. I pay homage to pens and paper and words in a way that I didn't realize the depth of my love, and curiosity for the written word, until I looked through the hundreds of poems that I've managed to write over the years. At times, I realize that writing has saved me. From what, I'd say losing my mind. But, at times, it also has messed up my life.

My first book, *Inside the Insane*, was a tell all on inpatient psych wards in Los Angeles County, coupled with a memoir of my battle with Bipolar II. I really put myself out there naked with my life story and went to town on my issues with mental health treatment. Unfortunately, when the government found out about my book, they immediately removed me from my job working in the hospital, and stuck me in a basement of headquarters in the Administrative Support Bureau of the Department of Mental Health. They left me to read policy and procedure binders that were stacked to the top of my cubicle as a punishment. No one was allowed to speak to me because I was known to be a whistleblower, and I had this copy machine beside my desk that was like Chinese water torture as people throughout the day would come and go to use the machine, and they would completely ignore my existence. It was terrible, and after six months of torture, I went out on depression leave, which really sucked because I couldn't collect a paycheck and went into credit card debt.

But, I was not going to let them get away with freedom of speech and freedom of press so I hired lawyers to go after them for retaliation. It all ended in a settlement, and I was offered a new job which I was excited about only to discover on the first day of work that I was re-assigned to another job in another dumping ground: Homeless Outreach Mobile Response Team. I thought the basement isolation job was bad but that was cake next to where I landed. I had to outreach chronic homeless people all throughout LA County and once again I became sick.

I remember one time I asked this guy that was living on a bench in China town if he thought he suffered from depression and he said, "If you were living outside for decades wouldn't you be depressed?" After hearing that I knew that I too was in a state of depression due to my surroundings, and made a point to do whatever I could to get out of that position. So in this case, my writing destroyed my career and happiness for many years. But I was also considered a hero and courageous which is nice and everything but, I can't help but write my truth, despite the fact it can be harmful. Like I said, my writing, despite the potential harmful ramifications always comes forth. It always wins.

On the flip side, despite the damage my writing did for my career, I was in a toxic relationship in my personal life but thankfully; I had my writing to release me from the pain. During that time, I wrote two books back-to-back, "*What Men Should Know About Women* and *What Women Should Know About Men.*" So thankfully although it was a rough time in my life, I had my writing to save me. When I look back it's sometimes embarrassing to read some of the stuff that I wrote but I have no regrets. I am grateful and thankful that I am able to capture moments and bring emotion to life on the page.

Then slowly, I started to grow a fan base online. A reader of my work that was a behaviour therapist contacted me, and wanted to write a book that tracked my subconscious mind in a conscious state through analysing my words and it was fascinating. The book, "*Screaming at the Void*" ended up winning a prize for most original concept in the IPPA Awards, which was cool. It came out around the time my father passed away so it was bitter sweet, and as a result; I was motivated to put together a collection of my favourite poems, "*Diamonds From The Rough,*" which I dedicated to my Dad. On the anniversary of his death the books arrived at my door, which was a sign that my Dad was with me so in that instance, it's as if writing connected me to the spiritual world.

"*Undressed*" is my most recent work which features my poetry with commentary. I wanted to try something new, and writing is a great creative platform to explore. Most readers seemed to enjoy my comments on my writing more so than the actual poems which was cool. It showed a layer to my life and mind that enhanced the work which was new and refreshing. Moving forward, I continue to write poetry but think I'll continue to add commentary here and there as needed.

So, six books and over a thousand poems later, do I consider myself a success? Not really, yet. But I bet the writer in my heart, mind and soul would think otherwise. Either way, I would be a failure if I ever stopped writing but I really don't have a choice. I know that without my writing a piece of my soul would die inside, and that's just not acceptable. And even if I wanted to quit or take a break, my writing wouldn't let me.

Like I said, without my writing I have ZERO!
End of Erica Loberg's

David Poulter – Talking To Myself
Coping with Schizophrenia

"Helloooo!" The voice echoed down the chimney. "Long time no see." It continued. *"What do you want?"* I replied. "The soot is building up." *"Another task?"* "Yes, I am afraid so." *"When must it be done?"* "Now would be a good time."

The sun was breaking through the clouds; beams of light shone through the dusty, cobwebbed windowpanes. I had already opened the wooden shutters. Well, I had been told to. The nights were still a little chilly, but the days were sublime. The trees crowded around the house in a friendly manner, decked in fresh, luminous greens. Blue smoke drifted from the glowing embers in the hearth.
"The ladders are in the barn."
"Really?"
"Yes, both pairs, the roofing ones are lying flat on old hay bales. You'll find the chimney brush and rods in an old, plastic fertilizer sack next to them."
"But why? Why must I do it? Yesterday I had to..."
"The fire has been lit all winter and into spring. The chance of a chimney fire is increasing..."
The voice boomed in an insistent, yet amiable tone.
"Yesterday, I was told I had to walk 2 miles down to the small, hidden valley and find the dead tree. You told me to take the bow saw, which branches to cut off and carry back. It was a very long way. I said there was firewood nearer."
"That was not me."
"So who was..."

"Don't forget the dying fire, put the embers on the brass dustpan and quickly clean the chimney. Then you will have your fire again, without having to relight it."
I opened the front door, squinting in the bright sunlight, the plants enticed me – a thick riot of colours clamouring for my attention; demanding for my caresses. But I had another important task to do and hurried towards the barn...

TALKING TO MYSELF

Everybody, I guess, talks to themselves: fragments of imagined conversations, possible future dialogues, contrived, planned excuses. Loops in thought. Surroundings trigger concepts. All of these can be positive or negative, emotionally.

As a schizophrenic I eventually started to try to "sort and manage" my thoughts.

Clinging onto logic, a deep precipice beckoned, as it still does, occasionally. Possibly I was lucky. For when the condition first developed I was living alone in a very secluded spot: an old cottage in Ireland. Summer had just arrived and I had no regular job.

I had just split up with my long-term partner, which had been traumatic, but on the whole amicable for both of us. Yet for the number of years we had lived in the area we had cultivated a garden, and had both had, and still do, an inherent love of nature.

The "madness" I descended into involved wild, spurious commands, but also obvious, sensible suggestions, all intermingled, juxtaposed. These voices led me on a chaotic, erratic journey.

Due to the fact I was the one who initiated the relationship break-up most of our mutual friends kept away from me, regardless.

So I was left to roam a relatively safe landscape: traipsing through woodlands, immersing myself in isolated streams, wandering in fields. Returning to the cottage in the evenings. Everyday, I was given a list of tasks to do. Weeks passed, I guess – I wore the same clothes, never bathed, my fingernails grew long. There was food stocked in the cupboards, and some vegetables and fruit growing in the garden. I ate very little. Looking back now I don't really have a definite timeline.

The "idiot" was there but the "savant" had yet to appear. A joke.

It is possible a number of things took me out of this "nose-dive". Firstly, I had studied Art at college: hours and hours of contemplation of landscape. And as I mentioned before, I had loved the area, prior to the onset of the condition. Therefore, large amounts of my time had been spent just looking at beautiful scenery, observing the colours, the depth, shadows, distance and perspective. A lot of my thoughts were naturally "blank" or just vision based. In addition, the feeling, the moods in connection with this "looking" were upbeat, buoyant, positive.

Also, as mentioned before, the voices I heard were not all necessarily telling me to do ridiculous things. Some were helpful. And since living a solitary life, in a rural area, one has to be practical and methodical anyway, certain directions and orders improved my life.

The trick was to argue back at first, selecting the most pragmatic ideas. And later, the practice of developing focusing, by continuously doing menial chores that were easy, such as sawing and chopping wood.

Next, constructing a routine. Enhancing positive impulses and voices. Programming reminders in my thoughts, attempting to make friends with myself. Ignoring as many negative voices as possible. Checking reality and facts against my deluded thinking. Reinforcement and positive feedback.

Writing now has become a habit. Something I cultivate, as I once did with my garden. An analogy: I endeavour to plant helpful, useful and constructive beliefs and ideas in my psyche. "Watering and feeding" them. Constantly weeding out the distractions and lies. It is not always easy, even now. Writing lists and notes has helped, such as reminders. Also creative project ideas and stories of experiences. Personal experience is everything and is difficult to communicate. Still, the process helps me try to understand my own condition. The further I push the boundaries of myself, in a gentle way, the more insights I get, hopefully. Certainties are not always certain. But certainly attempting to treat my surroundings and the people I meet with respect and warmth has helped calm down the illogical, unbalanced, impulses, voices and emotions.

Tim Price

My Name is Timothy John Price (Tim Price), I write to keep myself out of hospital. I was diagnosed with depression in 1990 and Asperger's Syndrome in 1994. I write to improve people's lifestyles and improve their abilities and capability and understanding of writing books.

I also do photography and art.

I write because I enjoy writing.

My first attempt was at comprehensive/high school. it was about politics I have not published this book. It was 72 sides of a four paper I threw it away and recycled it by mistake. The other children were playing outside while I was writing. Writing helps me relax. Relax, relax, relax.

I wrote a piece about my Uncle Tom when he died in 2010. My first book for Chipmunkapublishing was "How to improve mental health" which I wrote on A4 paper in 2012 which is the best book I have write in my opinion. I brought a laptop to word process.

My Dad helps me to write my books, he checks the work and proof reads it for me.

I am a Creative person, writing helps me to be very busy indeed, and it keeps my brain working and functioning. I need to keep doing things to keep me busy all the time because this helps me with my writing and to improve my mind and my education.

I have 7 books been published in total, they are:

How to Improve Mental Health,

My insight into the computing world,

My Middlewich about the town I can remember

The changing world of mental heath

Olympic Games London 2012.

The Rio Olympic games,

Improving care in the community.

I am always writing new books and my ideas for books are changing all the time.

I am writing my own Doctor Who book. I plan to publish 2 books as soon as possible writing is my main occupation now. I spend many hours each week on my books.

I have a website, pricetimj.com and business cards. I run a book writing business.

I give my business cards to lots of different kinds of people.

I should have started writing when I was 16 years old before I was ill with depression the first day I left school. I might not have been ill at all if I started writing but this is in the past. My other interests are photography and doing my artwork but writing is my main activity. I tell different people about my writing. I regard my writing as a full time job. Writing can inspire other people to write new books. I want to start my own writing academy one day in the future. This is one of my own objectives of improving my wring skills.

I advertise my books on Facebook, Twitter and my Website, with help from my Dad.

Writing gives me a positive outlook to my writing ability and writing skills writing. I would like more investment in my books. My writing gives the reader an insight into my how I write to express my feelings and improve my writing skills and writing knowledge.

I did not really think that I would become a published author it was only something to do instead of doing nothing, being on benefits, living off the state. One day I might earn enough to not live off benefits. This is my aim and the reason I invented my writing job in the first place. I am happy to be an author and proud of being published.

Nigel Pearce

On writing, the imagination and catharsis.

> I write only because there is a voice within me that will not be still.
>
> - Sylvia Plath,

Poetry is often written in isolation and the archetypal tormented poet driven to the edge of madness and beyond is typified in Sylvia Plath. Indeed, she was one of the greatest poets of modernity. However, for Sylvia Plath and the vast majority of other poets and, indeed, writers of prose this is not a chosen position, but it does require a meaningful interrogation. It cannot go unquestioned by those who write in the genre of survivor poetry and prose.

The genre of 'confessional poetry' can be understood to have begun in times of material affluence. The consumer boom' of the 1950s and 1960s. Of course, there had been poets writing in both great poverty and also living their life out in asylums. A famous example is John Clare who died in Northampton General Lunatic Asylum in 1864 after existing there for around twenty years. This poem he wrote while incarcerated in the Lunatic Asylum encapsulates the experience:

> I Am! BY John Clare.
> I am—yet what I am none cares or knows;
> My friends forsake me like a memory lost:
> I am the self-consumer of my woes—
> They rise and vanish in oblivious host,
> Like shadows in love's frenzied stifled throes
> And yet I am, and live—like vapours tossed
>
> Into the nothingness of scorn and noise,
> Into the living sea of waking dreams,
> Where there is neither sense of life or joys,
> But the vast shipwreck of my life's esteems;
> Even the dearest that I loved the best
> Are strange—nay, rather, stranger than the rest.
>
> I long for scenes where man hath never trod
> […]

Nevertheless, his poetry did not create a new mode of writing, as did Sylvia Plath, Anne Sexton and Robert Lowell.

Sylvia Plath rejected the nascent Beat culture, which would become the alternative scene of the counter-culture with its emphasis on induced altered states of consciousness. Poets like Allen Ginsberg and Elise Cowen and prose writers William Burroughs were significant Beat writers. Although Elise was probably ill when she met the others around Columbia University in the 1950s. Ginsberg's early and mould-breaking poem 'Howl' began:

Howl
BY ALLEN GINSBERG
For Carl Solomon
I
I saw the best minds of my generation destroyed by madness, starving hysterical naked,
dragging themselves through the negro streets at dawn looking for an angry fix,
angel-headed hipsters burning for the ancient heavenly connection to the starry dynamo in the machinery of night,
who poverty and tatters and hollow-eyed and high sat up smoking in the supernatural darkness of cold-water flats floating across the tops of cities contemplating jazz,

Their experimentation in poetic form and lifestyle became a resistance ideology in the 1960-70s. Sadly by the mid-1980s the 'scene' had degenerated into a myopic hedonism. The dream was over as cheap opioids and stimulants began to permeate society and were accompanied by an economic crisis which capitalism has yet to resolve.

Is there another way for the poet today? Yes, but the roots are very different. Rather than the isolated and tormented poet or the writer walking around with tombstones in their eyes, we can comprehend a path of social collectivity while preserving the unique voice of the writer. A Marxist aesthetician, Christopher Caudwell, argued:

> A poem's content is not just emotion, it is an organised emotion, an organised emotional attitude to a piece of external reality.

So, poetry as a genre is not just emotional prose. Rather it has forms which, of course, are there to be broken. A form that I often apply when I need to discipline my mind is the haiku. Try it for yourself and it will eventually help to order your thoughts.

The path ahead I allude too is called 'proletarian monism'. It was a theory developed on the far-Left of the Avant-garde renaissance in the early days of the Russian Revolution before the repression of free thought under Stalin and his new bureaucratic ruling class. 'Proletarian monism' was argued for by people like the early science fiction writer and doctor Alexandra Bogdanov, Boris Arvatov and the poet Mayakovsky. None of them would survive Stalin's terror of the 1930s one way or another. Boris Arvatov argued:

> Art and life – how should these apparently heterogeneous phenomena be connected to each other? The question is a stumbling block in front of bourgeois science and bourgeois practice, unsolved and unsolvable in the conditions of capitalist society.

Certainly, it can only be solved in a communal society where the artificial divide between work and creativity is resolved. For we are creative creatures who interact in order to transform one another and our means of subsistence when in a 'state of nature'.

Hence this school competed with many others who were debating art and literature in the early days of the revolution and called themselves Productionists. With the ambitions of eradicating the artificial division of mental/physical labour. Or as Alexander Bogdanov claimed, 'Is not the poet, the organizer of his class.' Bogdanov as I had mentioned coined the term 'proletarian monism'. This is essential to understanding proletarian literature and art. Bogdanov thought 'collective labour' and the consciousness produced by it was the foundation for a proletarian poetics. He argued that it: 'embraced every aspect of a human and embracing all elements of experience'. Thus, it counterposed 'bourgeois dualism' where there is not this unity but division. He argued elsewhere:

> To organize the forces in his social world, his struggle...the proletarian needs a new class art. The spirit of this art is the collectivisation of labour; it assimilates and reflects the world from the viewpoint of its feelings... its creative will.

Where does this leave the proletarian poetic aesthetic, Marxism? I agree with the poet Vladimir Mayakovsky, who worked for the revolutionary Left Front for the Arts. It must endeavour:

> [to] re-examine the ideology and practices of so-called leftist art, and to abandon individualism to increase art's value for developing communism.

To abandon the paths of either tormented self-isolation or self-destruction the ultimate solution is a society described thus by Karl Marx:

> In a higher phase of communist society, after the enslaving subordination of the individual to the division of labour, and therewith also the antithesis between mental and physical labour, has vanished; after labour has become not only a means of life but life's prime want; after the productive forces have also increased with the all-around development of the individual, and all the springs of co-operative wealth flow more abundantly—only then can the narrow horizon of bourgeois right be crossed in its entirety and society inscribe on its banners: From each according to his ability, to each according to his needs.

To achieve this is the task of the proletariat and their natural allies, the poets and writers of prose. Until we attain a communal society, we must put pen to paper in whatever way we can and write. Finally, in the words of the great French feminist and philosopher, Simone de Beauvoir:

> A day in which I do not write leaves a taste of ashes in my mouth.

Nigel Pearce: author at Chipmunkapublishing (PG. Dip. Humanities, B.A. Humanities with Creative Writing.)

Janet Qureshi

Writing helps me clear my mind. Renata Azman (now deceased) used to say "Don't keep it in your head, write it out, write it out, write it out."
May God bless her and may she rest in peace, she was a truly inspirational person and wrote several amazing books published by Chipmunka.
Personally I am so thankful to God that I can write about anything and everything.We are lucky to have the freedom that this country offers.
Thanks to Chipmunka my book "Aspects of Life" has been published and I have received great feedback.
I attend a "Readers' and Writers' group at the University of Birmingham (monthly) as part of Suresearch which includes Service Users and Carers, Practitioners and Academics who are all concerned with Positive Mental Health.
I cannot speak too highly of the amazing work that you all at Chipmunka do to remove the stigma surrounding mental health issues.
Long may you continue and long may we continue to show that "the pen is mightier than the sword."

www.ingramcontent.com/pod-product-compliance
Ingram Content Group UK Ltd.
Pitfield, Milton Keynes, MK11 3LW, UK
UKHW041413180426
11947UKWH00007B/107